African Safari

Izabella Hearn

T0385934

Level 1

Series Editors: Andy Hopkins and Jocelyn Potter

1.1 What's the book about?

Talk about these pictures. Where can you see these animals? Which animals live in your country?

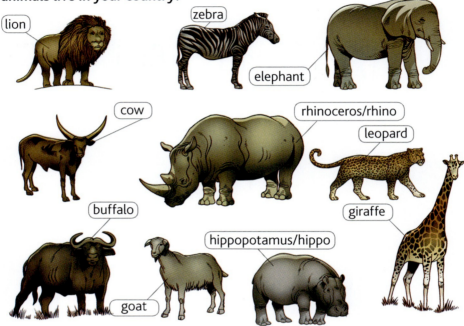

lion

zebra

elephant

cow

rhinoceros/rhino

leopard

buffalo

giraffe

hippopotamus/hippo

goat

1.2 What happens first?

1 Look at the new words in bold on page 1. What are they in your language?

2 Look at the pictures on pages 1 and 2 and underline the right words in these sentences. What do you think?

   a Adam and Lily are going on safari in *Africa / Asia*.

   b They want to *see animals / meet people*.

   c Joseph, an old friend, is waiting for them with his *plane / jeep*.

   d There are three American *visitors / students* with him.

   e Later, a *lion / leopard* has breakfast near their jeep.

African Safari 1

1

It is very early in the morning. Adam and Lily are going on **safari** in Kenya. Their friend Joseph is waiting for them.

Look, Adam. I can see him!

2

The aeroplane is arriving at a small airport in the Maasai Mara.

Joseph is standing near his **jeep**. He works in the **game reserve**. Today he is meeting Adam, Lily and some American visitors.

3

The friends say hello and get into the jeep.

This is Anne. Behind her are Jeff and his son Tom.

Hi! Is this your first safari?

Yes. I can't wait.

4

I know that face.

breakfast /ˈbrekfəst/ (n) I always have a big *breakfast* on Sunday mornings.
safari /səˈfɑːri/ (n) This *safari* is in Kenya. I often go **on safari**, because I love animals.
jeep /dʒiːp/ (n) You can drive on bad roads in that *jeep*.
game reserve /geɪm rɪˈzɜːv/ (n) There are a lot of elephants in Kenya's *game reserves*.

lucky /ˈlʌki/ (adj) She's a *lucky* woman. She's got a beautiful face and a lot of money.
danger /ˈdeɪndʒə/ (adj) *Danger*! Don't swim in that river! Swimming is **dangerous** there.
Some animals are **endangered**. Not many people see them.

The Big Five

Joseph loves his job. The day starts very early, at 5 o'clock. Every day he drives visitors across the Maasai Mara. Often, breakfast is in the jeep. They stop near the River Mara and watch the hippos. They see the giraffes in the trees. Families of zebras are eating **grass**. Then Joseph and his visitors look for the Big Five.

The Big Five are big, strong animals. They are lions, leopards, elephants, buffaloes and rhinoceroses. They are all very dangerous.

Lions and leopards usually **hunt** for food at night and sleep in the day. Lions hunt and **kill** big animals. They eat giraffes, zebras and **other** Big Five animals.

Leopards eat **meat** too, but they like to eat small animals. First, they kill them. Then they often take the dead animals up into the trees. There, they eat them slowly.

---

grass /grɑːs/ (n) It was very hot, but the *grass* under the trees was green.
hunt /hʌnt/ (v) Many people *hunt* animals for food.
kill /kɪl/ (v) He *kills* animals with his knife.
other /ˈʌðə/ (adj/det) I've got two pens. One of them is red and the *other* pen is blue.
meat /miːt/ (n) My sister loves animals. She never eats *meat*.

Buffaloes live in big **groups**. They are very strong and they can kill a lion. They eat green food: tall grass and other **plants**. They like the rain and they like to be near water. They live for about seventeen years.

Rhinos are endangered animals. There are only about forty black rhinos in the Maasai Mara today. Some people hunt rhinos because of their **horns**. In some countries,

people give a lot of money for a rhino horn. This is a big problem. The police and the **keepers** want to stop them, but that is difficult.

Rhinos eat grass and fruit, but no meat. They sleep in the day. Sometimes they sleep on their feet.

Elephants live in big family groups. They don't eat meat. They only eat trees, plants and fruit. They are very **intelligent** and they can understand other elephants. They make noises, but people can't always hear them.

group /gruːp/ (n) The teacher talked to a *group* of students after school.
plant /plɑːnt/ (n) These are new *plants* for the garden.
horn /hɔːn/ (n) Some cows have big *horns* on their heads.
keeper /ˈkiːpə/ (n) The *keepers* stay with their animals and give food to them.
intelligent /ɪnˈtelədʒənt/ (adj) Susan is a very good student. She is very *intelligent*.

2.1 Were you right?

Look at your answers to Activity 1.2 on page ii. Then finish these sentences.

> Adam and Lily are going on [1]................. . The game reserve is in the
> Maasai Mara, in [2].............. . Their [3].............. Joseph is waiting for them.
> He has got a jeep and he is going to be their [4]............. . Some American
> [5]............. are with him. They are all staying in the same [6]............. .
>
>   Suddenly, Adam hears a noise. A lion is having [7]................ . It is eating a
> [8]............. !

2.2 What more did you learn?

1 Are these sentences right (✓) or wrong (✗)?

    a The Big Five are all strong, dangerous animals.

    b Rhinos are endangered animals.

    c Lions and leopards sleep at night.

    d Elephants are very intelligent.

    e Buffaloes can't kill lions.

    f Rhinos sometimes sleep on their feet.

2 Write five sentences about the Big Five.

	eat	meat.
	don't eat	plants and grass.

    a Lions ....

    b ....

    c ....

    d ....

    e ....

2.3 **Language in use**

1 **Read the sentences on the right.**
Then finish the sentences below.

> Today he **is meeting** Adam, Lily and some American visitors.
>
> Tomorrow we**'re going to get up** at five.

Today

a Joseph and the Americans ......*are meeting*...... us at the airport. (meet)

b The plane .... early. (arrive)

c Anne .... very quiet. (be)

Tomorrow

d I .... hippos and giraffes. (see)

e Zoe .... to me. (write)

f Adam and I .... a lot of photos. (take)

2 **Finish the sentences.**

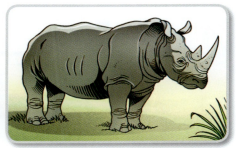

| dangerous big slowly | | quickly famous short |

a Elephants live in .... groups. They are strong, ... animals, but they walk ....

b Rhinos are .... for their horns. They have .... legs, but they run ....

2.4 **What happens next?**

1 **Talk about the pictures on pages 8 and 9. Why isn't Lily happy?**

2 **Look at the photos on pages 10 and 11. Where are these elephants? Why? What do you think?**

African Safari 2

A Long Afternoon

adopt /əˈdɒpt/ (v) The children have no mother or father, and the American family are going to *adopt* them.

I'm going to give £1 a week because I'm *adopting* an elephant.

orphanage /ˈɔːfənɪdʒ/ (n) She lives in the *orphanage* because her mother and father are dead. She is an **orphan**.

Adopt an elephant

This is Shukuru. She is from Tsavo. Today, she lives in the Sheldrick Elephant Orphanage near Nairobi. She arrived at the orphanage in September 2009. She was only three days old.

Now she has a new family and a lot of friends. Visitors can meet her. They can adopt her too, but she is always going to live in Africa.

A lot of people visit the orphanage. At 11 o'clock in the morning, the elephants come out with their keepers. The elephants run and play. Then the keepers give them their food. Sometimes a young rhino comes out and plays too. The visitors stand very near the animals and take a lot of photos.

The animals are in the orphanage because they haven't got families. The keepers are their 'mothers'. After some time (perhaps ten years), the elephants go back into the **wild**.

wild /waɪld/ (n/adj) In Africa you can see animals in the *wild*. These are *wild* animals.

Samson's Story

The year was 1954. There was very little rain in the Tsavo Game Reserve. Some visitors arrived and they loved Tsavo.

One evening, they watched a family of elephants. One young elephant was very thin and unhappy. He was ill and he wanted water. He walked slowly behind his mother. The elephants arrived at the water and started to drink. The young elephant wanted to stay near the water. His mother wanted to go. She didn't want to go away from her son, but she went with the other elephants.

The visitors watched the young elephant. He was lucky. No lions or other animals came near him.

The elephant was the first orphan in David Sheldrick's elephant orphanage. His name was Samson.

3.1 Were you right?

Remember your answers to Activity 2.4. Then answer these questions.

1   Who is the man in the photo?   ....

2   What is he doing?   ....

3   Why is the elephant there?   ....

4   Is the elephant always going to live there?   ....

3.2 What more did you learn?

Write these names in the sentences.

| Joseph   Adam   Lily   Anne   Jeff   Tom |

1   .... sees buffaloes, but wants to see elephants.

2   It starts to rain and .... stops the jeep.

3   .... isn't happy because she didn't want to stop.

4   Later, ... takes the group to a river.

5   .... sees an elephant with its mother.

6   .... wants to see the hippos, but first she looks at her phone.

7   .... looks at Lily's phone too.

8   .... buys rhino horns. Her name is Ruth Street.

3.3 **Language in use**

Read the sentences on the right.

> One young elephant **was** very thin.
>
> She **didn't want** to go away from her son.

1 **Which picture comes first?**
Write the numbers 1–4.

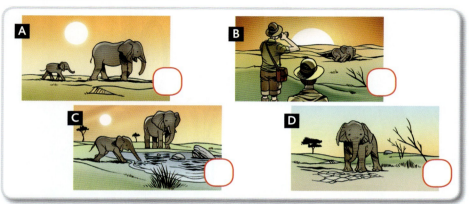

2 **Now finish the story.**

There ᵃ ..was.. (be) not much rain that year. The animals
ᵇ........................... (not have) much food. The young elephant
ᶜ........................... (be) ill and he ᵈ........................... (want) water. He
ᵉ........................... (walk) slowly behind his mother. They
ᶠ........................... (arrive) at the river and the small elephant
ᵍ........................... (start) to drink. He ʰ........................... (stay) at the
water for a long time, and he ⁱ........................... (not go) back to his
mother. Some visitors from the game reserve ʲ........................... (watch)
him. Not long after that, he ᵏ .... (have) a new family.

3.4 **What happens next?**

What is going to be in these two newspapers? Get some paper and write
one or two sentences. Then talk about the stories. Which story is right?
What do you think?

Police catch Ruth Street   **Ruth Street runs from police**

African Safari 3

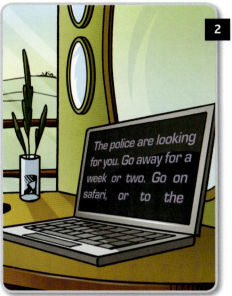

14

5

Can we get out?

Yes, the keepers are always near them.

Lily looks at the rhinos and thinks about Anne.

6

Smile, Tom!

Jeff is smiling too. He's got photos of four of the Big Five.

7

Thanks, Joseph. That was a beautiful day.

Leopards tomorrow, Tom, and Maasai dancing this evening!

Adam, let's find Anne.

8

She isn't here, and her things aren't here.

Where is she?

The Maasai People

The Maasai are very interesting people. Many live in Kenya, near the Maasai Mara Game Reserve. The men and the women are tall and strong. Every day, they walk across the country with their cows and their goats.

There is very little grass in the Maasai Mara, and very little rain. The men and boys hunt wild animals and bring them back home. Sometimes, very young boys kill lions. This is dangerous, but for the Maasai it is important.

The Maasai dress in beautiful colours: usually red. They like dancing and **singing**. Sometimes they sing and dance for visitors at the hotels in the game reserve.

sing (v) /sɪŋ/ The children can't sleep. I'm going to *sing* to them.

Maasai women don't hunt, but they do a lot of work. They build the houses for their families. The Maasai people move from place to place and the women build new homes in the new places.

Every morning, they get up very early and bring water for their families. This is a very important job because water is a big problem for the Maasai. The women make the food too. The Maasai eat meat and they eat food from plants.

Not all Maasai children go to school. Often there are no schools near their homes. School is expensive too, and many families haven't got the money.

Today, many Maasai people live and work in towns. Sometimes they visit their families and friends.

African Safari 4

A Good Day for Rhinos

Talk about it

1 **Work with a friend.**

Student A You are Lily (or Adam). You want to go on safari again, but Adam (or Lily) can't come. You ask Zoe/Dan, but she/he doesn't want to go. Talk about the animals and the people in Africa.

Student B You are Zoe/Dan and you are not happy about a holiday in Africa. Isn't it very dangerous? Do you get near the animals? Are you going to go on a small aeroplane? Is there a lot of walking? Ask Lily/Adam questions. Are you going to go?

2 **Work with two or three friends.**

Student A You are a policeman/woman. You have Ruth Street at the police station and she is answering questions.

Students B, C and D You work for newspapers. Ask the policeman/woman questions about Ruth. Is that her name? How old is she? What is she saying? What is she doing in Africa this time? What are the police going to do with her? When?

Write about it

Which of the Big Five animals do you want to write about? What do you know about it? Look at other books and on the Internet. Then write about it.

1 **You and your friends are in Nairobi. You want to go on a safari but you only have two days. Talk about these questions.**

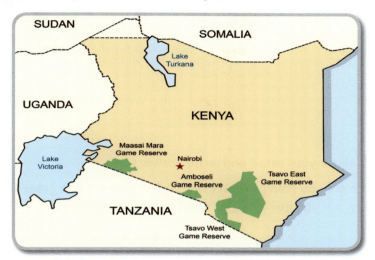

a Which game reserve are you going to go to? Find pictures of them on the Internet.

b How are you going to get there – by aeroplane or in a jeep?

c What animals are you going to see?

d Are you going to visit the Maasai?

2 **You want to see some or all of the Big Five.**

a Why do you want to see them? Talk about it.

b Are they all endangered? Why? Look in books or on the Internet.

Rhino	✔ (for its horn)

3 **Find out about these animals.**

	A	B	C
Name of animal	....	....	....
Food	....	....	....
Dangerous?	....	....	....
Endangered?	....	....	....

4 **Now talk about your safari and write answers.**

What time are you going to start the day? Where are you going to meet? How are you going to go? What do you want to see?

DAY 1

MORNING ....

....

AFTERNOON ....

....

EVENING ....

....

DAY 2

MORNING ....

....

AFTERNOON ....

....

EVENING ....

....

5 **You put a short film about your safari on the Internet. Write about it for your friends.**

Watch our film. It's about our safari to ....
We were very lucky. Here you can see ....
....
We ....
....
....